SEED KEEPERS

Also by Cynthia West

For Beauty Way, Poems, Inked Wingbeat, 1990
1000 Stone Buddhas, Inked Wingbeat, 1993
Rainbringer, Poems, Sunstone Press, 2004
The New Sun, Sunstone Press, 2007
The Seasons of Tea, Views and Poems, Blurb, 2010
In the Center of the Field, Poems, Sunstone Press, 2011
A Clear Drop, Poems, Sunstone Press, 2015
Visionary Paintings, Blurb, 2019

SEED KEEPERS

Poems

Cynthia West

SUNSTONE PRESS

SANTA FE

Cover Art: Seed Keepers, Cynthia West, 2006
Cover Design: Cynthia West
Title Pages: Cynthia West

Sunstone books may be purchased for educational, business, or sales promotional use.
For information please write: Special Markets Department, Sunstone Press,
P.O. Box 2321, Santa Fe, New Mexico 87504-2321.
Printed on acid-free paper

Library of Congress Cataloging-in-Publication Data

Names: West, Cynthia, 1942- author.
Title: Seed keepers : poems / Cynthia West.
Description: Santa Fe : Sunstone Press, [2023] | Summary: "Poems by a
   well-known Southwestern US writer and artist"-- Provided by publisher.
Identifiers: LCCN 2023033432 | ISBN 9781632935519 (paperback) | ISBN
   9781611397253 (epub)
Subjects: LCGFT: Poetry.
Classification: LCC PS3623.E843 S44 2023 | DDC 811/.6--dc2320230802

LC record available at https://lccn.loc.gov/2023033432

WWW.SUNSTONEPRESS.COM
SUNSTONE PRESS / POST OFFICE BOX 2321 / SANTA FE, NM 87504-2321 /USA
(505) 988-4418

DEDICATED TO MY FAMILY

ACKNOWLEDGEMENTS

My thanks go to the following publications in which the poems have appeared.

"In Both Worlds," *Sin Fronteras - Writers without Borders*, #23, p.66, editor, Ellen Roberts Young, 2019

"Water Wheel," *Giving Voice to Image*, Vivo Contemporary Gallery, 2016

"Shaken by Change," *Santa Fe New Mexican*, *Pasatiempo*, 9/20

"Become the Gift," *The Green Fire Times*, 11/20

Tanka, Gusts, editor Kozue Izawa, 2018–2020

Tanka, Moonbathing, a journal of women's tanka, Editor, Pamela Babuski, 2018–2020

I am most grateful to Able West for his patient, considerate corrections that clarified and deepened the poems. Many thanks to Kyce Bello for editorial assistance that increased the resonance and availability of the work.

What means the most in the creating of poems is collaboration with my poet friends. Many thanks go to James McGrath for teaching me through his masterful example. Writing with him provides a steady source of inspiration.

CONTENTS

INTRODUCTION

A BASKET THAT HOLDS SONGS

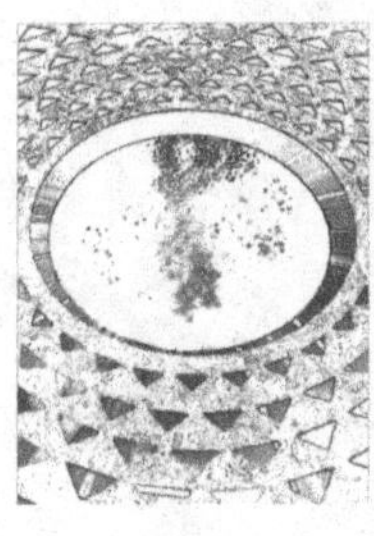

THE BEADWORK CODE

STANDING WITH EACH OTHER

THE BIRD WE DIDN'T HEAR

OPEN PASSAGEWAYS

INTRODUCTION

Cynthia West opens her book, *Seed Keepers*, with her cover painting, the self-portrait of the Seed Keeper: one who shares the gifts and beauty of a master gardener.

In her poem, "*Seed Keepers*," Cynthia admits speaking "with the voices of kind red foxes, the morning dew, the blue birds raising dawn."

Cynthia West is a master gardener of words and images. She shares what she has learned "from corn stalks rattling in the breeze, from evening rabbits, grey as the shadowed earth, from the murmurs of cedars and apple trees" in her poem, "What Sings."

This poet sings with her seed words. She selects an image, plants it in her heart-bed, nourishes it with soul-warmth, trims its excess, trains its flowering, cultivates, shares its harvest with us so we can celebrate together.

In her poem, "No Regrets," Cynthia gives us the invitation, "Let's keep running to catch the sunrise even as the days grow short."

Seed Keepers is a gathering of spirited, fertile seeds to plant in our own gardens as we till and praise the world we share with all living beings.

—James McGrath, Santa Fe, New Mexico poet

A BASKET THAT HOLDS SONGS

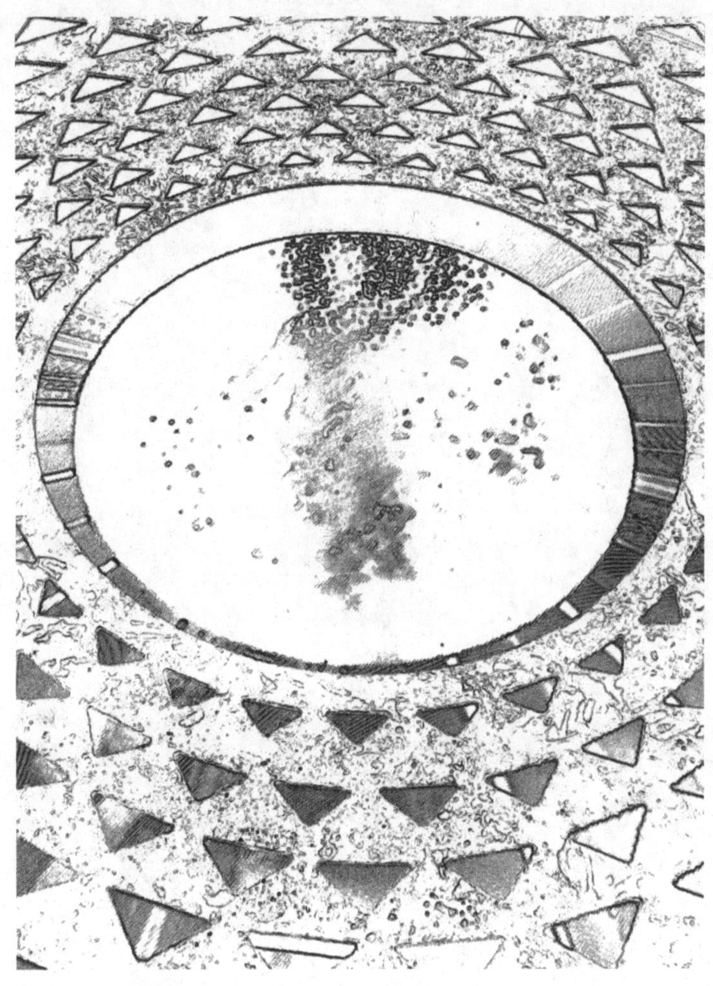

Become the Gift

Don't ask for anything,
        because more is being given
        than your heart can count.
Your elders urge you
        to become the gift
        you were sent to be.

They are fields offering more flowers
        than you can ever pick.
They remind you, your love is a well
        that can't be emptied.

Your old aunts and uncles
        plant you with knowledge
        carried across deserts at great risk.

Their medicines are candles
        they teach you to light.
Don't let grief keep you from acting.
Use it as kindling
        to ignite the wicks.

With Time for Each Other

At last we have fallen silent,
    without factories, cars, planes.
The air clears until every moment stands,
    no longer obscured by rush.

Plans drop away, canceled,
    leaving us to the terror
    of staying home with our shadows
    staring us in the eye.

Nothing to do but befriend
    the unwanted self who has been crying
    for our attention all these busy years.

We want to run from the stillness.
If we can stop inside ourselves,
    the change can happen.

We can receive the seeds
    that have waited for us to open.
    This is our clean new skin.

The Internet of Being

No one is looking, eyes fixed on screens,
    lured into virtual worlds by lies
    of future nourishment. Scientists who studied
    the stories of the skies sit lost,
    watching videos of clouds,
    shadowed illusions that dull the desire
    to pursue what used to matter most.

No one is looking as destroyers
    lift protections from the waters until river songs
    cease to flow between the banks,
    until birds no longer trill buds open.
    Nature's faces, with their tongues cut out,
    still speak the language of silence,
    passing pulses through root telegraphs,
    supporting one another.

Artists, musicians, poets -
    we who have always walked, invisible,
    unheard, seemingly lost,
    are creating colors that blinded eyes
    have forgotten how to see.
    We are communicating with flute notes
    through the internet of being.

Luminous moonlight rising from the desert,
    our music penetrates the waters,
    raising tides in every living thing.

Ropes of Light – Solstice 2020

Short days close around us, shadows
that long to birth something,
a water never tasted,
a filament of promise,
a pattern intricate as a spider's web,
as delicate and as strong.

The ropes of light we are forging
emerge from deeper in our bellies
than we have ever been.
Prayers the ancestors breathed
into our DNA flow in silken silence
gathered from the stars,
shining with the sun beyond the sun,
the source of all water.

Asking for a new way of being,
we spin multicolored threads to catch
the first rays of rising light.
Built of grasses and twigs, stained with
the juices of herbs, our fresh circuits
lead away from the old tales
that used to guide our feet.

They are the strength within the corn.
They are the story that waited until
the one we believed, ruined past use,
fell away, an outgrown shell.
They are the return of light
radiating throughout our cores.

An Open Basket

After years tightening each knot
    in my tapestry of doubt,
    it has unraveled.
The wind carries the strands
    across the field, drops them on cholla,
    limp threads tangled on thorns.
The grasses dance free at last
    under blue skies clear as water.

Taught to never let this happen,
    I've been relieved from the job
    of holding up the world.
 It's strange to be forced to stop,
    to stay home listening
    to the small child who never had
    a chance to be heard.

When wild plum blossoms join
    spring snow on the ground
    my path worn in the field remains,
    an open basket,
    no longer tied in knots.

Raven Mother

Slow now, in a dance with Raven Mother,
I'm a teenager courting an impossible love,
learning to give up everything
to be accepted in her flaming black feathers,
to drown in her fierce golden eyes.
Perched out of reach on wind-swayed clouds,
she regards my gifts,
years of planting and harvesting,
as not enough.

Trying to please her, I'm painting shrines,
ponds with water from my prayers
and lilies that weep when the moon is full.
I'm too busy to notice the wheels
of my days drawing us closer
as I build a huge statue of her
with many arms and mouths,
feathers shining black stars,
iridescent, the bones of forever.

Preparing votive candles from the wax of separation,
I melt in broken promises,
loved ones lost and songs pressed
from sweet night roses. I pour
the boiling oil into molds crafted
in the shapes of my days,
that she may accept me as I am,
no pretense, apples, peaches, a clear mountain view.

november flocks
wings dark then bright
this raven ritual
patterns the sky
for winter's steps

In Both Worlds

Holding me in her lap, my mother taught
        me borders. "You must forget the world
        where you live, and move into the one

where I am. You can't be free. You can't
        know. You have to quit flying higher
        than the pines". She modeled how

to appear blind, deaf, like all the rest.
        I passed in her world, appeared to be
        who she wanted - mimic, mirror, echo,

right appearance. Her lessons mapped
        where the borders were and weren't,
        allowing me to move between.

She has never paused to face
        how absent I am, laughing with the stars,
        playing marbles with river ripples.

At one with roots and bones, a skinless
        presence with no walls, I am a whale
        blowing spray from the depths into light.

I am brown earth all the way down,
        beating to the core. I am the sound
        of wings after the bird has flown.

Baskets that Hold Songs

Threaded to the days with laughter,
I played, dancing, trying on names like clothes,
sharing rainbows with the clouds,
hopping over stones
in the river of flowing hours.

My fingers have forgotten how to twine
bull rushes into baskets that hold songs.
My voice has lost the sound
that pleases the ducks, greens the frogs,
mingles with the face of the rising moon.

Kindling a campfire in a hidden canyon,
unroll old pictures bright as coals.
As the colors on the water fade to dusk,
the child I was calls a thousand cranes.
She has found the music of remembering.

The Mother I Never Knew

Before my warmth
        was taken from her body,
        she wove her name in my blood
        with starlight so I could see.

She put her feet in my feet,
        her dreams in my dreams,
        so I would never be as alone as her.

With aching breasts, she built me a house,
        filled the shelves with milk and honey,
        arranged kindling on the hearth,
        piled firewood outside.

She mapped my path, marked my way
        hoping I would never be lost.
        Lessons were prepared for me;
        friends positioned for when I hurt.

Her tears still water the garden of lilies
        she planted in my smile.

moonrise
over white mountains
reflects in the river
intimate
as we used to be

The Water Wheel

Six years old, tucked into bed, I drift
        as my mother reads. Snow buries
        our country home. The fire sinks to embers.

Her voice, a river of story, carries me
        to dreams, wheels turned by the pages
        of memory. Secret words inside the folds

slide between my waking
        and my sleep. The lamp-lit current
        of her rhythm rises, falls, quiet

in the winter dark, a warm honey
        weaving us together with the night,
        wheel upon wheel, revolving,

each page, remembered meaning, her face
        mine, my face hers. As I slumber,
        the water lifts, circles, then pours down,

comforts my small body with her sound,
        safe, warm, story with no end,
        water turning round and round.

Last Night Gazing

A child, last night gazing,
became the moon. The moon became her.
Inside the moon were all the men and women
who lived before,
the ones who made her with sticks
and cornmeal. The ones formed
of bark, leaves and feathers.

Last night gazing, she became the sea.
The sea became her. The moon spread
a road of light across the water to her feet,
lured her to follow. One step
after another, held by the silver path,
she arrived with the ancestors
who guarded her red cord.

Last night, she was a turtle preparing
to birth the stars. Gazing indigo galaxies,
she swam, flipper-strong, fluid,
knowing where to burrow,
where to loose eggs, when to let
the dark tide carry her to the next release.
Last night she was the moon.

Learning the Footsteps

Last night gazing, she joined
the ones who went before,
a circle of fire and cedar
singing chants made of raindrops
gathered before time changed the world.
Learning the footsteps laid down
in patterns, she moved with the rhythm
of many voices weaving.

THE BEADWORK CODE

Seed Keepers

Our ancestors brought us here to remember
    the clay of the fields, the water of the rivers,
    the fire of the sun, the clarity of the air.
Their clear-eyed songs saw through the aeons

as they wove circles around the central tree,
    calling the earth's ancient peace up
    into our future bodies so we would dance

their prayers forward. They fanned our breath
    with eagle feathers so it would speak beauty.
By washing their shadows with melted snow,
    they ensured we wouldn't repeat their mistakes.
With the colors of their blood, they painted

our bodies, that in the turning wheel of years
    we would share their knowing of the cedar trees,
    the mother corn. We would speak with the voices

of kind red foxes, the morning deer, the bluebirds
    raising the dawn. The coded beadwork seeds
    they sowed in our cells were set to wake us
    when the right hour would arrive.

The Old Eyes

The destroyers who consume the earth,
the trees, the water and all life forms

aren't able to possess
what they can't understand,

the honey beyond price
that we are growing to be.

Let us stare with the old eyes of stones.

Another Winter Dusk

Pushed by shadow, late golden light
climbs the mountain. Patience rests
under snow. You, the earth, angered
by our arrogance, could shake us off.
We wouldn't feel your footsteps
passing over our dust.

Let us have a few more days,
the solitude to offer circles of prayers
garlanded with wild grass.

Let us pour water on your wounds
and each other's. Let us sing the songs
we learned from roots that feed
the stones upholding the sky.

Let us have time to complete
our portraits painted with tears and laughter,
the thousand shades of friendship.

Let us light candles in the dark,
that we may never forget
the shining music that rings our bodies
the same as it does yours.

All Souls Eve

Because the strength of our bone ladders
reaches back to the first fire,

we have always built
welcoming beacons

to lure our ancestors across
the silver moon waters.

They rush, swifter than currents,
bird flocks wheeling, wings

shifting from black to white.
Together again, no one remembers

how many times the leaves
have fallen gold, or how often the sky,

reaching down through branches,
has swallowed us.

With No Words but the Language of Faith

Ancestors, every time you pressed your foreheads
     to the earth in prayer
     a rose bloomed.

Centuries before I would be born,
     on a far away mountain,
     you seeded my body.

The merging of your brow and the ground
     wove garlands,
     twined green dwellings on my path.

You taught me to dance, built it into the body
     you would never see
     in a future past your understanding.

With your love flutes, you played knowing
     into my bones before they existed,
     gave me the name of the rose to discover.

weaving today's pain
on the loom
I reconnect
severed arteries
between people and nature

Spring Run-Off

Coyote rides the wild wind-horse of spring,
    with no direction, no pause, catapulting
    through unknown lightning groves,
    her home turf. The unexpected, her daily bread,
    fuels her velocity, connecting energies

that blast from the tip of her tail to her nose.
    With no center, no front, she is roots
    sprouting roots, an arising flow, wonder
    surging up the trunk of the world tree.

Coyote, a swift arrow, delights
    in unmapped paths leading nowhere but here,
    the beginning that is always,
    the sunrise that warms seeds,
    the light that births birds at dawn.

Corn Planter

The circle of loved ones supports her hum
    on the trail inscribed in the fertile earth.
    The Elders standing in the four directions
    hear with the ears of the clouds, with the patience

of standing stones. After listening a long time,
    they have felt the heights above and
    the depths below infuse her body
    with the sound that sprouts seeds.

Ceremonies have dug a spiral.
    Cornmeal offerings have prepared the ground.
    Prayer sticks guard the field.

The Elders return her beaded doe-skin bag,
    guarded for millennia. She is Corn Planter,
    a vision deer. Her hoofs and rainbow-edged antlers
    sweet as water from melted snow, tall as the pines,
    remember the ancient way.

Blood beat, river pulse, lung wings, resound.
    Singing the same as corn, as earth
    her fingers insert the first spark
    to be held, protected,
    fed in the drumming womb.

Generations reaching through her small hands
    plant, cover and bless each earth-blue,
    fire-blue, water-blue, sky-blue seed into its spot.
    The sun blazes; millions of spirits sing.

Open Pathways

Our bodies are shrines built from years
    of planting seeds in the earth,
      climbing mountains and sharing friendship.

Their colored flags are sewn with clouds
    racing through blue sky.

Their open ceilings are pathways to the stars.

We prepare roads for the weary,
    provide bowls of water for travelers to drink.

Corn, beans, flowers and fruits
    flourish in the small folds

that open between moments,
    offering nourishment that transforms
    suffering into the desire to serve.

The swallows dipping and diving at dusk
    are happy to be our guides.

STANDING WITH EACH OTHER

Desert Song

During the desert walking years
	with no shawls of kinship
	to guide us, we followed the sounds
	of colors, dark whispers, pearl turnings.

Lost, unable to read ancestral maps,
	we strained to hear where we were going.
	The wind dissolved our fragile
	sand dwellings. We forgot how

to listen to the resonance of cliffs,
	arroyos, thorns and ravens. Worn down,
	without melody, our faces fell away,
	step by step, until naked, we could see

the land that had been calling.
	Able at last to answer the thunderers
	booming our names, the leaves
	greening in unison, the earth

humming us forward, we remember
	we are the water that sings,
	the eye, the source, the ocean,
	the full moon of lighting our way home.

The Teacher
to The Teacher

Once, we lived on the breathing earth
where all voices understood one another.
The choice of speaking or being still
was stolen from us
by people who could only make noise.

When they swallowed our tongues
the hawks hid and the crows
ground blackness into bitter flour.

By starving us of the music of sunrise,
they hoped to turn us
into masks with no purpose,
feet with no direction,
like theirs.

But we were built differently,
blood, bones, minds printed with patterns
that matched the turning earth.
We knew the speech of being, the one chorus
colored through millions of mouths,
the song underlying song.

With our volume muted, the stories
that formed our bodies had no wings to fly.
Deprived of air, we could not breathe.
Until the teacher's full listening
melted the stitches
that had sewn our mouths shut.

One of our kind who cared,
who recognized our value,
kindled the watch-fires waiting
on the ridge lines of our memories.

One person who had ripped
their own chains loose,
who had refused the canned prison meat,
who could sing with the wild grasses
throwing seeds to the wind,
changed our minds.

One moment of being heard
was enough for our suns to start rising.
We escaped bondage,
allowed our voices to stretch
into stories long denied.

It only took the slightest opening
for our cobwebs to dissolve,
for our wounds to heal,
for our pollen, potent from long restraint,
to be unleashed.

Sacred Water

Sacred water surging up our stalks
prints patterns in kernels growing
on cobs of red so deep
it's black with the potency
of life condensed.

Holding hands on the spiral path
our verdant bodies rustle in the breeze.
our faces smile, old beyond old.

Two Old Women

to Priscilla Hoback

Refugees from families who raised us
    to know nothing,
    we dared difficult desert crossings
    to recognize these high mountains
    as the promised land.

Mouths open wide, we drank deep
    of the milk and honey.
Young then, everything was real.
Living in old adobes,
    we weathered howling winds
    as rainbows came alive.
We asked the clay we dug from the riverside
    to become vessels that would serve.

The kneading, pushing, pulling rhythm quieted
    our minds to hear rain falling on the window.
In the gentle flow of creating,
    our hands spread friendship to the earth
    that shaped us in turn, taught us
    to sing together in the silent way,
    clear as water, strong as mountains,
    free as hawks riding thermals,
    centering motionless in blue wind.
Together, our clay-gnarled hands,
    wise from digging roots,
    from soothing children,
    offer the chalice we were given
    to each other's lips.

Horse Woman Visits

to Brynn McKay

One neigh from the horse-woman
was all it took to set us throwing laughter
and red rose petals around the kitchen, waking
the winter house to joy. She had driven down
from Colorado in a blizzard,
blasting through a snow-white tunnel road.

The kitchen resounded with warm cooking
of beans, corn and deer. As the storm slid west,
golden light broke under the clouds,
shining through the windows.
All it took was her prancing over to the stove,
weaving stories brighter than the new moon.

Forgetting the sixty eight years since
I felt like a horse,
I'm running out the door with her,
into the icy cold, with no destination.
Women, animals, no thoughts, no concerns,
we gallop the sleeping fields,
piñons, cedars, rabbit tracks,
now an ocean.

Star field horses leaping over arroyos
wonder-lost with speed, we cast
red rose petals across the ice bound hills.

What Is Tea?

to Natsuko West

The distance the sunlight
shining on the table has traveled
to warm this afternoon
leaves no trail.

Tea is the smile you give me
when we bow.
Sorrow unfolds into promise,
melting grey snow
into the mud that feeds roots.

Tea stops the roar of the wind.
In the quiet respect that arises,
the blue heron spreads wide wings,
flies south.

Tea is sharing
earth, air, fire, water.
In the beauty that has no words,
we are a lake without ripples
where the whole moon floats.

No Longer Small

Seeing faces in the clouds,
I find friends who feed honey
to the side of my mind
that hides, except in dreams.

At the feast we share songs
with the wind and the hawks,
laughing until rain descends.

When everything has a face
my face becomes everything.
No longer pale with small wishes,
it is bright with all creatures, plants
and mountains.

Beyond the limits of names,
I'm no longer a dammed river,
but the oceans that circle the world
with one blue understanding.

Listening, I can feel my way
to the places inside my eyes
where the clouds tell stories
that bridge life and death.

As a quiet winter day ends,
my form is no longer the center,
but an offering given,
able to plant seeds
in other hidden minds.

Invited to the Table

to Benjamin and Rabia Von Hattum

In the rose garden, white butterflies serve
    brown bread, yoghurt, orchard fruits.
Blue birds burst from mosaics on the walls -
    color, pattern, honey. We are no longer in the grey room
    waiting for the doctor who does not heal.
Fed by the table, the jam, the tea, the laughter,
    we fill each other with songs.
We are wild grasses offering seeds to each other,
    cloud shadows bringing rain
    to the curves of red earth.

The sunlight shines on our cheeks,
    swallowing our fears so gently
    that death doesn't matter any more.
As the beads of moments slide
    through our fingers, we climb the mountain
    gathering everlasting flowers.
No one cares that our hair is silver. No one
    counts the tears of grief shed
    to ignite our candles into torches.
When the snow falls, our white butterfly wings,
    unable to be apart,
    will beat together with the sky.

In the Gold

to Susan Yanda

Truth wears clean water,
    no obstruction,
    just the color of no color,
    simple, translucent, ringing.

It has the fragrance of sun-lit air,
    clean sheets on the line in spring wind,
    wave froth settling into sand,
    the undersides of stones that no one visits.

Truth says what doesn't want to be heard,
    what doesn't want to be done.
    Truth speaks with the gold
    of which the heart is formed.

It eats peaches in hot September,
    earns a living by being free.
    It dreams the world into being -

from tiny bugs, to huge mountains,
    to the fires people kindle
    so they can gather
    together in song.

At the Hospital

As the new moon sets through apricot blossoms,
I walk into your room, confused.
Dark now, the blood in your brain
presses nerves so your arm can't move.

The girl you were is gone
with the deer on the hillside.
Can you begin again
when forty-three years have passed
and the little rabbits that spoke to you
are far away now?

We have only
the days that are given
to be together.
May we not pass with our heads down,
but rejoice in the trees,
in the flashing sunlight we can't catch.

We have only our faces,
naked in the light,
only the words
we say to one another,
only the moments,
our green smiles,
our branches leafing out.

What Sings

Since our mothers and fathers
        didn't know how to teach us to sing,
        we've learned from corn stalks rattling
        in the breeze, from evening rabbits,
        grey as the shadowed earth,
        from the murmurs
        of cedars and apple trees.

Dusty sunsets give us songs
        trembling with the winds that dance
        around dried weeds. Flocks
        of crows echo our sounds
        until we hear the light singing us.

The hills, the valley, the river
        leap with harmonies
        our voices could never raise
        until we understood
        they weren't our own,
        but shared with all life forms.

when you showed me
how to see a star
in the morning sky
I never guessed
you could disappear as fast

THE BIRD WE DIDN'T HEAR

Damaged Mitral Valve

The house of the heart
    with its four worn rooms
    labors alone on the river in the rain,
    roof cracked open
    allowing a view of the sky.

Lost in survival,
    that wet and broken organ
    has forgotten how to stop.

Wearing a torn coat,
    the fluttering valve,
    in a cage the doctors can't repair,
    cries with high-pitched fear.
The current rushes, swollen,
    dissolving blame.

With no need for reasons,
    the small boat continues
    beating as if it were whole.

To My Doctors

You can't tell me how small I am any more.
    The illnesses you claim I have
    are not where I live.
They are traps
    without space for the wonder of new grass.

It has taken many years to recover
    from your efforts to reduce my crimson petals
    to some diagnosis you can medicate.
    Now that I don't listen to your line,
    each sunrise ignites my lost becoming.

You can't tell me how sick I am any more.
    The road doesn't end
    where it disappears around the corner.
    Rather, it continues
    until it meets its beginning.

Walk out into the mystery before dawn.
    Tell me where the leaves and the air
    begin and end. Tell me where you begin and end.
    Reach up through the sky,
    your fingers will never stop touching.

You can't tell me how terminal I am any more.
    No longer held in clay, I'm not concerned
    about my earthen vessel breaking.
The force that breathes my flesh, blood and bones
    knows how to join the singing wind.

The Answers I Need

The wild tiger is what I want most,
    each organ free,
    bones that stand with no confusion,
    nerves singing their own clear song.

You'd suppose I could follow
    the tracks of the cat inside me,
    a certain presence, strong with sun.

Stripes and eyes appear
    through dappled forest foliage,
    only to disappear.

Thinking I can't find her
    is all that keeps us apart.

If I dared to dive
    into the hot belly that holds
    the answers,
    I would drown in change.

After a Diagnosis

Start a dialogue with the predator
    that waits to consume you.
    Admit your wounds.

Let them show. Ugly, they are the road
    you built to the garden of tears and laughter.
    Stand exposed, in each hand

the power to act. Connect the wires
    they told you not to join. Complete
    the circle, seen/unseen, light/dark,

until your circuit runs strong
    with fish sliding silver under the surface.
    Thank the disease for reminding you,

death is an open door. Sit on a stone.
    Speak the sorrows wanting
    to be heard. Learn to navigate the path.

Draw a map so the ones coming after
    can find the far horizon
    with the green sun brighter

than a thousand dawns. Let the body
    you were wearing vanish
    like sunlight through branches.

A Flash Flood

A flash flood rips away the stories
we think we have become. Listening,
we hear the ground we built
rush down the river
carrying branches torn from trees.

Diving the Change

Under the raven's wings,
we are new birds, our black feathers of night
dissolving into the brilliance of dawn.

Our invisible ears are starting
to connect to the lines
between trees, rivers and mountains.

We fly foolishly, unaware of stones
or the bridges built of them. Playing
sky currents, leaping, diving,

we test the edges of change.
There are openings that allow
vision beyond our small eyes,

largeness beyond the years.
Unconcerned about losing our way,
we plunge in, washed of all we know,

fresh as juniper branches
in the fragrance of summer rain.
No one expects us in this shape,

cawing with grand laughter.
From perches on power lines
above the fear-shrunk world,

we enter the cloud houses
of the dancers who raise life.

It is not the energy doctors measure but
the water of the sunrise in one being
becoming the water of the sunrise in another.

Ravens fly in the raging wound
as well as in the silence
beyond peace.

Our job is to peck sparks of light
from the sun then place them
in the empty aching holes.

Basket of Wonders

to Zachariah Rieke

held between black orbits
     anywhere but everywhere
natural canvas portal   shadow-dance
   the deep going through   black energy tracks
basket of wonders

atomic garden rainbow hum
   bugs above the trees   thunder clouds
what's really going on
     a magnet moth dust wings opening
   closing slowly
rain-sound   water entering water

brushstroke severs illusion   pure force finality
   utterance of an ancient sage
the unreachable touched   dark and light

smell of charcoal ground black soot
   my small drowning makes no matter   no story
can be heard   in the night ocean
    clouds trees leaves float none stays

how small it is to be
   in the wind of stillness the motion of power
     how small it is to be among great forces

The Small Grey Stone

When you think you need something
you're not getting, your mind has stolen
the bright distance, substituted a mean grey
with neither here nor there.

When the wind has blown away your walls
leaving you alone, you can't feel sure.
Your mind has separated you
from living in wholeness until you do not see
the small stone at your feet. Pick it up.

The white line across it is a mystery
that can't speak as long as you are hiding
from emptiness. Let the river of moments
wash you clear as the swift running clouds.

Take the small stone home.
Place it in your palm. Ask it for the language
your bones know. Let your eyes return
to the warm afternoon. Find yourself
in the moment that never leaves.

The sun shining on your cheek
welcomes you back to understand
how you were fooled into forgetting
you are the same water music
that rings in every person.

Keep the grey rock near.
Remember, you can never be without.
You have all you want to give.

despite the virus
ending life as we know it
cottonwoods
along the river
offer golden leaves

OPEN PASSAGEWAYS

No Roads

To learn how to reach
    the country with no roads,

climb a mountain
    every day. When yellow leaves

pattern the wind, you will be given
    new feet that know how to travel

through change. With your hands
    empty from letting go,

prepare for departure by cleaning
    the windows, maintaining

the shrines, becoming the nothing
    required to enter the sky land

with no need for a body. Stand by
    the river thanking the water

that carries your face
    in fast, shining ripples.

You Taught Me to Gather

to James McGrath

After you leave I will trace
your footsteps on the dirt road
by your house. Matching my pace
to yours, I'll learn to mingle rhythms
with the paths of rabbits, owls
and rattlesnakes. After you leave

I'll join the black horses snorting
in the mud. In the water trough,
I will view reflected memories
dropped by passing clouds,
the kind you taught me to gather
from moments between tears and smiles.

After you leave I'll count
the fence-post's shadows, for they mark
the many years you listened
to the whispers of the old ones
carved in stone up on the ridge.

They will give me stories
because I follow in your tracks,
remembering to tell the ways
the undersides of rocks
keep meaning alive
when no one knows.

To the Artist

Artist, there are no maps
        for out beyond the mind,
        so you draw your own.

Reweaving nerves
        into gardens, you coax roses
        from the mud.

You think nothing
        of the possessions
        left at the dump.

With no flashlights
        but the candles blazing
        in your eyes, you seek

pearls that can't be bought.
        Your smile builds bird-houses
        from the bones of the stars.

After A Summer Rain

The river leaps
over stones.

The hand that reaches
through currents
retrieves nothing
every time.

The willows laugh,
understanding
what can't be held.

Every Morning

Every morning, washing the blender
    after making our health drink, I watch
    the wind blow sunlight through the weeds.

Reaching the sponge
    down to clean the blades
    with warm, soapy water,
    my mind slides through concerns
    that the world as I know it has changed.

Every day the view is the same,
    an apple tree, the wind waving wild grasses,
    the play of light and shade.

My same feet stand on the brick floor,
    my same body washes the dishes
    as it has for fifty years and my same eyes
    watch the sun rising over the same hill.

While lost in scrubbing, without a thought,
    I feel no need to be anyone
    but who I came to be.

Gratitude

Gratitude is the music of atoms ringing
    in and out of formation,
    the music of sand grains sliding
    inaudibly through one another.

It is the breath between notes,
    the dark matter between stars,
    the nothing that holds everything together.

Love is the rhythm and beat of blood,
    bones, fire, water, a river of snow-melt
    rushing to nourish the earth.

It is the joining of pulses, the mingled resonance
    arising from leaves, birds, stones, seasons,
    oceans, all life forms, praising as one.

It is frequencies weaving the carpets
    that warm the paths of wholeness.
    It is the flute, flying ahead, messenger.

Gratitude is adobe mixed,
    the bricks of days and pains
    laid one atop another.
It is the corn harvested, the food offered,
    the wounds washed, the tears shared.
    It is the walls that hold nothing out.

Love is the place of meeting,
    of hearing the voices of grasses and herbs,

the merging of colors, the giving of secrets,
the hidden and the regained.

It is the Source Spring in plain sight, seen by few,
lost and found from moment to moment.

The Moon's Eye

Loosening my hair, I bend my head
into the spaces between
currents woven to the shuttle's rhythm.

Back and forth in and out hot cold light dark
humming patterns emerge songs
of the one long thread

that carried me here
that will carry me back.

Night day fast slow in out
asleep in the cadence
awake in the dream

silver hair longer
than the moon's eye
staring from a winter sea.

Soon to Leave

We've lost count
of the swelling and thinning moons,
so many years
here on the land
we have called our own
under the patient mountain.

Soon to leave our home
to wander unfamiliar valleys,
we stay to help each other die.

What I Leave

Not much sand remains
        in my hour-glass.
It is late in my long painting
        of seventy-five years.
The colors of my blood
        flash light, then dark,
        spinning, funneling
        into a flaming crown.

When my skin, eyes, bones
        return to the field
my prayers will live in you,
        written in love,
        readable only by love.
My freedom coat
        will fit all of you.

The colors of my blood
        flash light, then dark,
        spinning, funneling
        into a crown of flames.

What I leave is every kiss
        I planted in you so deep
        it will continue
        long after you are gone.

Notes that Are Beads

When I am no longer here,
walk the river for me.

Sheltered in adobe walls, warm
from the care of many hands,
chant with the garden drum,
dance the steady beat of seeds
sprouting underground.

Fill the bowls I spun from clay
with corn and beans you've grown.
Honor the empty spaces
they hold, my dreams
of simple home-made days.

Enjoy the photos stored in closets,
the slides, the paintings
of bright stars dancing up mountains,
of rainbows germinating the earth.

Sing my prayer-song, notes
that are beads strung from walking
the canyon, shaping the earth,
weaving visions into birds
with wings strong enough to fly.

This Tiny Boat

What if the sunlight falling on the table
becomes a road for my feet to travel
away from the desperation of this afternoon?

What if the table becomes a boat
and the sun an ocean with no shore
anywhere in sight?

What if my breaths become oars
and row over gigantic waves,
chased by lion clouds
across a sky so new it hurts my eyes?

What if none of my precautions can save me,
none of my remedies return good health?
What if I let go the oars and trust
the green winds to carry my small vessel
where it is meant to go?

What if I'm woven together with the ocean,
without doing a thing? What if my avoidance
of death turns it into a constant companion
goading me to run after a non-existent pot of gold,
the rainbow long gone?

What if dying doesn't matter at all?
What if the ashes of loved ones offered to the sea
are a shining roadway, of which I am a part?

my painting chair

filled with yellow ash leaves
alone in the rain

Thanksgiving

For the longing that has lured us across deserts, over mountains, through
    loss, agony, aloneness…we give thanks.
For taking away and for putting back…*
For breaking our hearts into completeness…
For our imperfect bodies, senses and understandings...
For leading us to stand firm, so we don't fall when our foundations
    shake...
For emptying our houses until we can walk without fear…
For cleaning us with pure water until we are windows to let the light
    shine through…
For friends and our remembrance of them...
For the lands we travel that teach us the wholeness of the earth and its
    people...
For those who have hurt us, causing us to understand why we cannot
    inflict harm…
For the illnesses, the limitations, the restrictions that have forced us
    to give up our little selves…
For the freedom that does not come and go...
For memories rich with beauty, grief, passion, loved ones lost...
For this moment, our family gathered hand in hand around the table
    laden with the harvests we have brought to feed one another…
For continuance, our children, grandchildren, corn, apples, beans,
    squash…
For our circle of support, understanding, forgiveness, compassion…
For the trainings, tests, trials and warnings given to prepare us
    for the days that are now upon us…
For weaving our fibers strong enough to resist the fierce winds…
For joining us together in the wisdom that we grow from the One
    Root…
For the love to continue to sing, dance and drum
    the Tree of Life into bloom...we give thanks.

* Repeat, "We give thanks."

The Bridge Between

Whether we like it or not
we're being carried away from the world of form
by a river thrusting all we cling to
from our arms.

Our last glimpse of certainty vanishes
as we're rushed under the bridge
between old and new.

Clear voices inside of ourselves
call our names, causing us to forget
the words to songs that have lost
their meaning. The torrent catapulting
us forward along with uprooted trees,
is the new music, fire mingled with water,

the sound beyond death. Fearless,
washed clean, we release the need
for human shape. In the meeting inside
our eyes, there are no more eyes,

only stars spinning stately circles
inscribed on the heavens
by the compass of love before life arose.

In this dying no death can find us,
no desire can stop us. We are swept away,
no longer waiting to arrive.

we can only be
daylight for each other
as the dusk deepens
into the time beyond
the one we call home

Winter Solstice

The house I knew is gone,
replaced by a view
my heart can see
only at its most quiet.

An immense vista,
neither strange nor lonely,
promises friendship. Since I am willing
to listen, bare branches carry
my breath up to join
wheeling circles of doves.

This is what I was running after
without knowing how to catch up.
It is larger than my body kneeling
by the river, drinking water
lit by the rising sun.

No Regrets

With the old world ended,
    the new not yet begun, we have nothing
    but pure light and the laughter that turns the stars.
    Let's keep running to catch the sunrise
    even as the days grow short.

The seasons are turning so fast,
    there's no time to mourn the broken mirror
    that no longer displays the picture
    we thought of as reality.

It can't be stuck back together because
    the glue has run out, along with the reasons
    we forget that we are built
    of the same energy as everything else.

Let's sing melodies no one
    has ever heard. Let's be morning glories
    blooming on the first day of autumn,
    with faith our seeds will continue,
        fed by water from unseen springs.